9-96

W9-BCV-668

Encyclopedia of

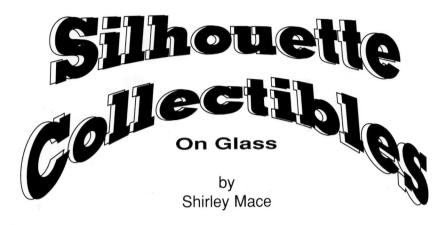

Silhouette Collectibles

On Glass

by
Shirley Mace

A beautiful book, in full color

Edited by
Marlys Sellers

Photographed by
Ray Mace

Printed in USA

Published by Shadow Enterprises
P.O. Box 61
Cedar, MN 55011-0061

The current values in this book should be used only as a guide. They are not intended to set prices, which may vary from one section of the country to another. Auction prices as well as dealer prices vary greatly and are affected by condition as well as demand. The author, publisher and printer do not assume any responsibility for any losses that might be incurred as a result of using this guide.

Additional copies of this book may be ordered from:

Shadow Enterprises

Shadow Enterprises
P.O. Box 1602
Mesilla Park NM 88047

$24.95 each

Library of Congress Catalog Card Number: 92-085393

ISBN 0-9633674-5-5

Dedication

This book is dedicated to the memory of my grandparents,
Carl and Hilda Helleckson. My Buddies.

Acknowledgements

A very special thank you to Chuck and Marlys Sellers and Ron Boerboom for all your advice, encouragement, and help in making this book a reality.

To the librarians who extended their services: Joan L. Clark, Mrs. Martin Frenk, Valerie Szalai, Kim Tenney, and especially to Barb McKie from the Benton Harbor Public Library.

I also wish to thank the following people who contributed in many ways:

Don Barth
Dean Brabec
Mavis Bratten
John Buckbee III
Mary Cardey
Dish n Dat Club
Robert & Mary Ellen Domeier
Sharron Freitag
Penny Engle
Richard & Debbie Gourley
Rich & Myrna Hammer
David Hoopman
Larry Hoopman
Lorraine Hoopman
Steve Hoopman
Barb Holland
Guy & Yvonne Johnson
Shirley Johnson

Lynn Knudson
Angela Kjellberg
Brian Kjellberg
Harry Kjellberg
Victor Miller
Helyn Presser
Joan Pudney
Marcia Rice
Jerry & Karen Richter
Marv & Pat Richter
Gary & Cynthia Schoonover
John Schultz
Mary Ann Schum
Cloie Smith
Jerome & Sally Weiler
Judy West
Bob & Casey Zollman

Introduction

Silhouette pictures as defined in this book are the colored pictures that are painted on the back side of the glass. This is also known as reverse painting on glass. They are usually black, but white, red, blue, rose or a combination of colors is also used. The subjects include children, couples, birds, dogs, horses, etc. Silhouettes have been used to decorate dishes, canisters, lamps, and many other items.

The backgrounds were usually paper or foil; sometimes textured, tinted or with scenic depictions. The backing behind this background is usually grey or black cardboard.

The hangers are sometimes attached directly to the glass; some may be a metal hanger that is attached to the back of the cardboard; some have a cut in the cardboard (meant to be folded out), with a hole for hanging.

Silhouettes were sold in variety stores, dime stores, novelty stores, or given as promotional gifts from the 1920's through the early 1950's.

Pricing

Prices listed in this book were determined by a survey of collectors, dealers, auctions, and others who purchase and are interested in silhouettes. Prices may vary considerably by region and availability. This book is intended to be used as a way to identify silhouettes and as a guide. Prices tend to increase dramatically on rare items, salesman samples, and due to the increasing numbers of collectors. People are becoming more aware of the value of silhouettes; the fun of hunting for a picture to pair with the one they have and the thrill when they find it.

All prices listed in the price guide are for perfect examples. Pictures which are less than mint condition are of less value than perfect examples. Damage such as scratched glass, rusted frames, missing hangers, or anything which may cause it to be somehow different from the original will lessen the value.

How to use this book

In order to identify, organize, and list all of the various manufactures, dates, sizes and styles, I have devised an abbreviation code. Example: BG68-24 will indicate BG = Benton Glass, 68 will refer to the glass size = 6" x 8", and 24 is the individual piece number. PW4d-1 would be Peter Watson; 4" diameter glass; and the 1 would be the inventory or individual number.

Frames differ in sizes and styles, therefore all measurements given are sizes of the glass. Measurements have been rounded off to the nearest half inch.

Some of the pictures have labels giving information about the manufacturer, date, copyright, etc. Without being too repetitious, I am trying to include most of the actual information through use of photographs and written information. Information which as been quoted from the pictures will be found enclosed in quotation marks. Unmarked pictures will be included in the section with the pictures they most closely resemble.

There are possibly many different companies which I have not learned of at this point in time. Any help in identification of individual silhouettes and/or manufacturers would be greatly appreciated.

Contents

Section One – Flat Glass

Contents

Section Two – Convex Glass

Section One
Flat Glass Silhouettes

There are several styles of silhouettes done on flat glass. They include round, oval, square, and rectangular shapes. The frames may be wood, metal or plastic.

The silhouette is reverse painted on the back side of the glass. In some cases there is a solid silhouette. Others are an outline painted on the glass and the outlined figure is then filled in with a colored tint. In the type using a tint, the background is a textured foil, (usually silver). The background on some is painted (usually a gold or cream color); some are scenic views of the outdoors, others may be any combination of the three.

This section includes some examples which I do not consider true silhouettes. They are reverse paintings on glass and are painted in color. They may only have flesh tones for exposed skin or may be in full color, including the trees, grass, and sky.

Some of the examples are silk screened, others are hand painted.

Dried wild flowers were used to enhance the background and provide color in some examples.

Advertising can be found on a number of the silhouettes and a few are souvenirs of various places. The advertising silhouettes often include a calendar and sometimes a thermometer.

This section also includes a few pages on Tinsel Art.

Plaster examples are also included in this section. They are not reverse painted on glass, although some were manufactured by the same companies. The figures are slightly raised above the surface and then painted as silhouettes. They are not framed, but have a border painted around the outer edge.

Silhouettes are not confined to pictures. They can be found on many interesting things. This section includes photographs of a number of different items which have been decorated with silhouettes. Some of those depicted are lamps, canisters, china, etc.

Art Publishing Co.
2509 Cermak Road, Chicago, Illinois

This company was in existence during the 1930's. Silhouettes and reverse painting on flat glass with details, tints and foil backgrounds are characteristic of this company's product. They made pictures primarily with Mother's verses, flowers, and human figures. These silhouettes were generally framed with wood frames and were very colorful.

Several of the examples have stock numbers on the backs. There are some which are dated (these dates are shown below the photograph).

The silhouettes below are a matched pair. The colors are painted on the glass with foil behind the tinted areas, to give the shimmery effect.

AP 710-12

AP 710-13

1996-97
Price Guide
for

Encyclopedia of

ON GLASS

by
Shirley Mace

edited by
Angela Ekvall

The current values in this book should be used only as a guide. They are not intended to set prices, which may vary from one section of the country to another. Auction prices as well as dealer prices vary greatly and are affected by condition as well as demand. The author, publisher and printer do not assume any responsibility for any losses that might be incurred as a result of using this guide.

ISBN 0-9633674-0-4

Printed in USA

Published by
Shadow Enterprises
P.O. Box 1602
Mesilla Park, NM 88047

SILHOUETTE COLLECTIBLES ON GLASS
1996-97 PRICE GUIDE

The silhouettes shown in my book are from several collections and most were made in America, hand painted or silk screened on glass. These pictures were popular for home decorating from the late 1920's until the mid 1940's. I started collecting in the 1960's and started doing research about 1984.

To everyone who has asked for more information, I am working on another full color book. I have received information from other collectors about some of the pictures shown in my 1992 book. A special THANK YOU to all who have written to me. I enjoy getting letters and appreciate when you send a self-addressed stamped envelope and your phone number when requesting information. I try to answer all letters in the order received but please be patient. Sometimes I am traveling, have other commitments or need to do some research to find an answer. I still have many unanswered questions but I guess there will always be some mysteries.

Silhouette prices are continuing to increase according to my last survey. The silhouettes are very hard to find in some areas. "They sell as fast as we put them out" is the most common answer I get when asking for silhouettes in antique shops. Quite frequently I am told that one of the dealers also collects silhouettes. Don't be discouraged, bargains are still to be found. I don't mind paying top prices when they are in excellent condition but expect lower prices on damaged pictures.

The convex glass or Benton Glass silhouettes seem to be the most popular. There is also a lot of interest in the wildflower silhouettes and I have included more information on these. Favorite topics are; children, western themes, and romantic couples.

Current prices for the silhouettes shown on the covers of the 1992 book should be as follows:

Front Cover: 6" x 8" Benton Glass $40 each.

Back Cover: Tin foil reverse painted picture of squirrel $20.

- Reliance Products, signed Smith Frederick is a 9" x 12" size and should be $38.
- C. & A. Richards . . . round flat silhouettes $15 each.

Section One

Page 10 .... Art Publishing Co.
See page 11 photos AP 810-19 and AP 810-20. I have been told by other collectors that this is the original foil background.

Page 14 ....Buckbee-Brehm Company
I have not been finding as many silhouettes painted on glass but more printed on paper by this company.

Page 20 ....Deltex Products Company
Many of these silhouettes are found in both in 8" x 10" size and the 4" x 5" size.

Page 24 ....Fisher Studios
Fisher Studios was started by Marion R. and Mary Fisher out of their home in Tacoma, Washington about 1926. During 1931 they moved the family and business to Oakland California. Mary Fisher was the artist who designed and painted the silhouettes. They also made coffee tables and trays with milkweed and other wild flowers in the background. Poems or "mottos" were sometimes added to the pictures. The business was closed after the start of World War II. One of their logos was a plain "F" inside an oval

made of curled lines. The other logo has a more embellished "F" inside a small diamond shape, inkstamped on the brown paper backing. I believe the diamond logo is the oldest. See examples below.

Page 26 ....Flowercraft Picture Company
Starting in the late 1920's, artist Nina Ferris hand painted silhouettes on flat glass with black paint. The backgrounds were made of milkweed "silk" and other wild flowers which had been tinted with paints. The company logo was an artists palette with 3 brushes as

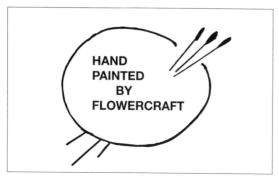

illustrated. I am still looking for more information and the date of the closing of this company.

Page 27 ....Forever
I have learned that this was a "line" sold by Newton Manufacturing of Des Moines, Iowa during the 1950's. Most of these have a clear plastic frame but I have found some with wood frames.

Page 69 ....P. F. Volland
I have not been lucky enough to find any more silhouettes from this compa-

ny. If anyone has some that we could use for our next book, please contact me.

Page 78 ....RF 5D-7
I recently saw this picture made with a real butterfly wing background in Texas for $30.

Section Two

Page 92.............Benton Glass Company
The process to make the convex glass was explained to me by some of the people who worked at the factory in Benton Harbor, Michigan. The flat glass was painted using a silk-screen, then set in molds and put into an annealing oven. When it was hot enough the glass would form into the shape of the mold.

This method also makes the paint very durable as it is actually baked on. These can be taken apart to clean and repair. I only recommend washing them if you are sure they are Benton Glass and not hand painted. If in doubt, don't take a chance. I damaged two of mine while experimenting. The plaster frames were used in the earlier years but were too easily broken. Metal frames were common and wood frames were considered "Deluxe."

Shadow Enterprises now has replacement hangers for the Benton glass pictures at .40 cents each plus .50 cents for shipping and handling for each order. Send orders to Shadow Enterprises, Box 1602, Mesilla Park, NM 88047.

To replace missing hangers, you will first need to remove the cardboard backing. In one corner of the metal frame there is a small tab. You will have to straighten the tab enough to slide it through the slot in the frame. The corners are flexible enough to open the frame and carefully remove the glass. The cardboard back should have a slit about 3/8 inch wide and about one inch from the top edge. Next, insert the new hanger with the hole on the outside of the cardboard backing. Pull hanger through the slit in the cardboard to the place indicated by arrow (see diagram below) Then you will bend the hanger up to help hold it in place. At this time you can clean the

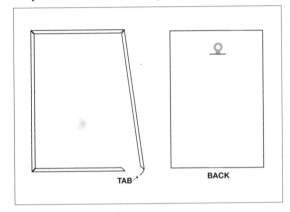

TAB   BACK

glass and re-assemble the picture. It is best not to open these frames more than once because the little metal tab can break off if it has been bent too many times.

Page 142.....................Bilderback's, Inc.
    I have been told that city directories were not published from 1942-1952 because of the war. A friend in Michigan found a 1941 listing for Ray Bilderback and a 1953 listing showing him as manager of a picture framing business at 20926 Schoolcraft, Bilderback, Inc. I don't know the name of the artists or the years that they were painting the silhouettes.

Page 143.................Edna Lewis Studio
    I have learned that Baltimore, Maryland was the original location of Edna Lewis Studios. After teaching art for several years, Edna attended Columbia University to get another degree. She started painting the little silhouette pictures in her home in 1932,

but had to rent a building and hire help to keep up with the orders in 1934. Reverse paintings in colors are shown in my book, but she also did hand painted, black silhouettes on convex glass. She sold her business in 1945. I have a copy of one of her catalogs and will give more details in the next book.

Page 144.............Peter Watson's Studio
    I have verified that Detroit, Michigan was the location of Peter Watson's studio. Peter Watson was listed as a commercial artist here in 1935 and 1940. These reverse paintings and silhouettes are hand painted on convex glass. Most examples are round with only a paper tape frame but I have found several ovals and one square with a wood frame.
    One of my friends in Michigan, Paula Lovett, sent me a roll of SCOTCH PHOTOGRAPHIC TAPE that she recommends for repairing the round pictures when the original paper frame is in bad condition. It is 1/2 inch wide, pressure sensitive, black opaque and is easy to work with. I tried it and with just a little practice you can get a very nice effect.

Page 149.........................Miscellaneous
    The four pictured are from Benton Glass with the original plaster frames.

Page 151
    One picture from Ohio Art Company is shown on this page. Ohio Art started making metal picture frames in 1908. I have a copy of a catalog from 1939 showing some of the silhouettes that I had originally listed as Benton Glass in my book. The catalog shows the following pictures were sold by Ohio Art: page 94, BG 68-7B & BG 68-8B; page 103, BG 68-111 & BG 68-112; Page 122, BG 45-81 & BG 45-82; page 129, BG 45-165 & BG 45-166; page 134, BG 45-187 & BG 45-188. It is possible that the glass was painted

and shaped at Benton Glass then shipped to Ohio Art for frames but I cannot document this. The owners of these two companies were friends as well as business associates. None of these pictures are marked but I have others that have "Ohio Art" embossed into the cardboard on the back. I didn't find anyone who used to work at either company who could explain this. In the future I will list any shown in the Ohio Art catalog as "Ohio Art" and specify if they are stamped with the name on the back.

Page 152
The 5" x 7" convex glass silhouette has advertising and a cardboard frame. I have found several others like this and they were sold by Stanwood Hillson Corp, Brookline, Massachusetts. This company was listed in 1927 until 1966 but I expect the silhouettes were from the 1930's and 1940's only. I am looking for additional examples from this company.

Section One
Flat Glass Values

Section Two
Convex Glass Values

* Not a pair

Page 138	BG 45-201	$40	Page 146	PW 5D-7	$25
	BG 45-202	$35		PW 5D-8	$20
	BG 45-203	$35		PW 6D-9	$25
	BG 45-204	$30		PW 6D-10	$25
Page 139	BG 45-205	$27	Page 147	PW 5D-11	$25
	BG 45-206	$27		PW 5D-12	$25
	BG 45-207	$27		PW 5D-13	$25
	BG 45-208	$27		PW 5D-14	$25
Page 140	BG 45-209	$30	Page 148	MC 5D-1	$25
	BG 45-210	$30		MC 9D-2	$25
	BG 45-211	$28		MC 5½D-3	$18
	BG 45-212	$28	Page 149	MC 4D-4	$20
Page 141	BG 45-213	$24		MC 4D-5	$20
	BG 45-214	$24		MC 3½D-6	$20
	BG 68-215	$22		MC 3½D-7	$20
	BG 68-216	$22	Page 150	MC 7D-11	$25
Page 142	BI 9D-1	$35		MC 7D-12	$25
	BI 6D-2	$20		MC 4D-13	$25
	BI 6D-3	$20		MC 4D-14	$18
Page 143	LE 9D-1	$18	Page 151	MC 2½23½-15	$25
	LE 4½D-2	$15		OH 45-1	$18
	LE 4½D-3	$15		MC 46-16	$20
Page 144	PW 57-1	$30		MC 45-17	$20
	PW 57-2	$30	Page 152	WP 4½5-1	$30
Page 145	PW 5D-3	$20		WP 4½5-2	$30
	PW 5D-4	$20		MC 57-18	$30
	PW 5D-5	$15			
	PW 5D-6	$15			

More information on other types of silhouettes may be found in the following publications: *Silhouettes: A History and Dictionary of Artists,* by Mrs E. Nevill Jackson. This book has 300 illustrations and features information about late eighteenth and early nineteenth century silhouettes.

Beauport Museum Collection Silhouettes, by Elizabeth Clay Blanford. This is a booklet of 21 pages with 13 black and white illustrations. The museum in Gloucester, MA has a collection of more the 60 silhouettes of various mediums.

The Public Museum and Art Gallery in Reading, PA has a collection of reverse glass paintings which include some silhouettes.

Dover Publications, Inc., 31 East 2nd Street, Mineola, N.Y. 11501 has over a dozen books with black and white silhouette illustrations.

AP 3½5-15
This picture is dated "Feb. 21, 1934" on the back side.

AP 810-19

AP 810-20

The cardboard backing on this pair is original and is marked "Stock #268", but I am not sure the foil background is original.

AP 710-1
This picture is stamped on the back "Stock No. 290"

AP 58-3

AP 710-7

AP 58-9

AP 812-5

AP 812-11
Signed on back "Best wishes for your
birthday April, 1936"

13

The Buckbee-Brehm Company
Minneapolis, Minnesota

The Buckbee-Brehm Company was at one time a part of the Bureau of Engraving. It was in business as early as 1927 and was listed in the Minneapolis City Directory until 1930. The latest date I have found on one of these silhouettes is 1931.

The characteristics of the silhouettes are: romantic couples; a name or quotation in a little title ribbon, at the bottom of the picture; copyright stamped on the back; Buckbee-Brehm stamped on the metal hanger. They did some silhouettes on plaster. A few of the silhouettes made by Buckbee-Brehm have a space between the glass and the background, creating the effect of a shadow behind the silhouette.

They made pictures in several sizes ranging from 4" x 5" to 7" x 10".

BB 4½5½-5

BB 4½5½-6

These examples are stamped on the back
"© By Buckbee-Brehm Company, Minneapolis, Minn."

BB 710-26

BB 710-28

The two pictures above are simply black and gold with wood frames. (Note the title ribbon in the lower corners.) The company name is stamped on the brass hanger pictured below.

BB 46-3

BB 46-4

"© Buckbee-Brehm Co 1930" Typical, painted on glass silhouettes.

BB 57-8

BB 57-9

These two silhouettes are made on 1/2" thick plaster and are the same pictures as their counterparts above, although they are unmarked.

BB 68-10

BB 68-12

The two pictures above are also 1/2" plaster, without frames and unmarked.

BB 4½6-7
3/8" thick plaster, in original box.

Logo on the box lid
"A Buckbee-Brehm Creation"

BB 46-14
This example is unmarked

BB 46-1

BB 46-2

The frames on this pair are slightly different. One is dated "1932" and one is dated "1933". This is a matched pair. "© Buckbee-Brehm"

BB 57-24
unmarked

BB 710-20
These pictures have the original metal
hanger, as shown on page 15.

BB 710-22
This picture has the Buckbee-Brehm
trademark and is dated 1931.

Deltex Products Company
Brooklyn, New York

The Deltex Company made flat glass silhouettes with foil backgrounds. The foil is silver or gold, matching the frame. The foil is slightly tinted in some pictures. The two sizes I have found are 4" x 5" and 8" x 10".

The Deltex Products Company was in business during 1933.

Deltex pictures have titles on the back of the picture. They also have information about the mate to the picture and most are stamped with the company name.

DE 45-26
"At the Gate"

DE 45-25
"Gallant"

The pictures above have the glass spaced approximately 1/4" from the background, so that it creates a shadow.

The silhouettes to the right would be a matched pair, except that one has gold foil background and the other has silver. They could be purchased with either.

DE 810-1 Silver
"Hearts"

DE 45-27
"Blossoms"
"Blossoms" has a reverse loop for hanging. The back has a message: "Drawing by a well known artist and painted on the glass. This design pairs with 'Hearts'. No. 048 Series Deltex Products, Brooklyn, N.Y."

DE 810-2 Gold
"Lovers"

DE 810-7
"Senorita"

DE 810-21

DE 810-5

DE 810-23

DE 810-15

DE 810-19

DE 912-11

DE 810-3

Fisher and Flowercraft

I have very little information on these companies. Fisher used two different emblems on the backs of their pictures. There is one picture which says it was made in California, with California wildflowers. This is very similar to the wildflower backgrounds done by Fisher and Flowercraft.

Fisher:
Fisher silhouettes were made with real, dried wild flowers pressed in the background.

At the time of this printing we had not found the location nor the dates of manufacture. These silhouettes are black, hand painted figures done on flat glass. Also see tray #1 on page 83.

FI 44-1

To My Mother
My best ambition
is to be,
What your dear love
expects of me.

FI 4½7-6

FI 44-2

FI 57-3
unmarked

FI 57-4
unmarked

FI 55-7
"Fisher Hand Painted Silhouettes"

FI 44-8
"This picture is made in
California with California Wild Flowers"

Flowercraft:

Flowercraft is another name found on the same type of pictures.

All of these examples are marked "Hand painted by Flowercraft"

FL 3½3½-3

FL 410-1

FL 410-2

Forever

The only information on this company is a trademark "Made in USA" and "Forever". Their silhouettes were available with a calendar and were often advertising pieces. My examples have calendars dating from 1950 to 1956. All of the examples I have seen have plastic frames.

FO 4½5½-6

FO 4½5½-3
1950 Calendar attached

FO 68-8
"Patented 'pulldown' calendar", calendar dated 1956.
The blue and gold are painted on the glass and the
pictures are placed behind the glass.

Newton Manufacturing
Newton, Iowa

The Newton Company is still in business. It was interesting to visit the company and see several familiar pictures in their diorama. The plant manager was nice enough to show us around the plant, but no one remembered making silhouettes.

The specialty of this company is advertising. Some of the pictures have advertising on the front and some on the back. They may also have poems on the back. They frequently were presented with calendars. Thermometers were optional for an extra .04 cents each, as you can see by the price list. Calendars may have been optional at some time also.

Many had a fancy, tasseled cord on the back for hanging. Beware of flaking paint, rusting frames and missing calendars on this type of picture. All examples I have seen of the Newton pictures, are on flat glass and have metal frames.

Some of the descriptive names used by this company are Art Silhouette, Art Shadowette, and Glass Art.

The photo of the salesman's sample shows a price list on the back of a 1939 calendar. The black, red and yellow colors on this sample are silk screened on the glass and have a foil background. One of the examples pictured has a 1961 calendar, so the time frame I have been able to document is from 1939 to 1961. The printing shown on the front is "Just another 'Thank you' Chas. Sprenger, Conger, Minn."

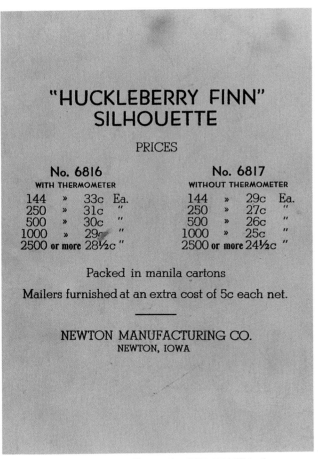

"HUCKLEBERRY FINN" SILHOUETTE

PRICES

No. 6816 WITH THERMOMETER	No. 6817 WITHOUT THERMOMETER
144 » 33c Ea.	144 » 29c Ea.
250 » 31c "	250 » 27c "
500 » 30c "	500 » 26c "
1000 » 29c "	1000 » 25c "
2500 or more 28½c "	2500 or more 24½c "

Packed in manila cartons

Mailers furnished at an extra cost of 5c each net.

———

NEWTON MANUFACTURING CO.
NEWTON, IOWA

Back of Salesman's Sample NE 5½7½-1

NE 5½7½-1

NE 45-2
"Made by Newton Mfg. Co.
Newton, Iowa"

NE 68-3

NE 810-4

The photographs above are excellent examples of Newton work. The top picture shows the metal frame, with some rust and flaking, (as is often found), around the front of the silhouette. The bottom picture shows the back of the silhouette with the verse, the cord and tassel and the advertising.

NE 68-5
"Made by Newton Manufacturing Co.
Newton, Iowa"

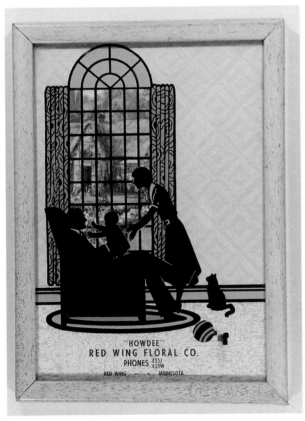

NE 57-6

NE 68-7

NE 810-8

The back of this silhouette has both a verse (including the author's name) and advertising as shown below.

1951 Greetings

This Art Shadowette

Presented by

Afdem's Cash Market

Blooming Prairie, Minnesota

Mother

The noblest thoughts my soul can claim,
The holiest words my tongue can frame,
Unworthy are to praise the name
More Scared than all other.,
An infant, when her love first came,
An adult, I find it just the same;
Reverently I breathe her name,
The blessed name of Mother.

– George Griffith Fetter

NE 68-9
" Days of Yore"

NE 48-10
1952 Calendar

NE 68-11

NE 45-12

"Made by Newton Manufacturing Co."

NE 45-16

NE 45-17

NE 57-18

NE 45-19
"Souvenir-Yellowstone Park, Wyoming-Haynes, Inc."

NE 48-20

NE 57-14

Butterfly Wings

Because so many morpho butterflies were collected for use in making ornamental trays, pictures, and jewelry the Brazilian government intervened for their protection. The beautiful colors are caused by the unique structure of the wings. The colors appear to change from blue to violet to brown as the picture is viewed from different angles.   The two round examples are on convex glass and the other two are on flat glass.

BW 3D-1
"Guaranteed made from real butterfly wings"

BW 57-6

BW 4½4½-4
"Guaranteed hand painted & real exotic butterfly wings Made in London"

BW 4½D-3

Reliance Products

Reliance Picture Frame Company from New York and Chicago
1820 Milwaukee Ave., Chicago, Illinois
Harry H. Wise, President & Registered Agent
Irving S. Roth, Secretary

Reliance was not listed as an Illinois Corporation until 1940. They remained on the list of Illinois Corporations until 1956. It appears, from information on the backs of some of the pictures, that they were, in fact, in business in Chicago in 1932. Some of the Reliance pictures are signed "Smith Frederick". To date, I have not been able to find information about an artist named Smith Frederick.

A large number of the pictures from Reliance have a stamp, similar to a postage stamp, on the back. The stamps have a blue eagle. "NRA Code" and a number are in red. "Issued by the Picture Moulding and Picture Frame Code Authority" is printed in blue. NRA are the initials for the National Recovery Administration, started by President Roosevelt. These stamps were used to show that the employer was in compliance with the NRA regulations.

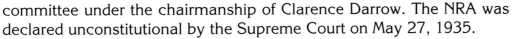

The purpose of the NRA standards was to end the price cutting and wage cutting spirals. An investigation was conducted in 1934 by a special committee under the chairmanship of Clarence Darrow. The NRA was declared unconstitutional by the Supreme Court on May 27, 1935.

The following two paragraphs are on the back of nearly all Reliance pictures: *"These truly beautiful creations are done in an exclusive hand process (right on the glass) exactly duplicating the world famous "Butterfly Wing" pictures. The delicate colors transferred directly to the glass present a pearly quality which makes them spring to life, and the glass itself seems to radiate an elusive light. Nothing has ever been offered before in America with such fineness of line, detail and rich coloring, and the "Butterfly Wing" effect process creates a brilliance not to be matched by any other type of decoration. In these very modern frames they will do credit to any room, and are particularly attractive when hung in pairs."* Reliance marked the backs of the simulated butterfly wing pictures with a B.E. and a number. Many of their other pictures had a T and a number.

Reliance produced a series of children's nursery tales silhouettes. Jack in the Beanstalk is shown in this section of the book along with a list of some of the other pictures in this series.

The pictures which have their original backs have a name for the silhouette on the back and frequently the name of the silhouette needed to make a matched pair.

RE 711-1
"Country Simplicity" paired with "Swan Pond"

RE 711-2

RE 810-15   RE 711-4

Printed on the back of the upper right picture is the following:

No. 420

This is one of a series of world famous children's nursery tales, and is reproduced in full color on glass. The brilliant coloring is uniquely transferred by hand in rich enamels, preserving a full sharpness of detail. The complete range of subjects are:

"Goldilocks and the Three Bears"
"Jack and the Beanstalk"
"The Old Lady Who Lived in a Shoe"
"Alice in Wonderland"
"Red Riding Hood"
"Cinderella"

Another "Reliance" Product
New York   R.P.F. Co.   Chicago

RE 3½5-17

RE 3½5-18

RE 912-20
NRA Stamp "12-33"

RE 912-19
"Beauty Secrets"
paired with "Vanity Fair"

RE 710-21
"Butterfly wing Effects-Hand processed
on Glass"

RE 710-22
NRA Stamp "12-33"

RE 3½4-25

RE 710-23

RE 711-33
"Double Dutch"

paired with

RE 711-34
"Tulip time"

RE 711-35
"Old Fashioned Garden"

paired with

RE 711-36
"Blossom Time"

RE711-40
"Autumn Bouquet"

NRA Code Stamp "12-33"
paired with

RE 711-41
"Phlox and Asters"

RE 711-42
"Autumn Bouquet"

RE 711-44
"Autumn Bouquet"

These are the same pictures, different colorations used.

RE 3½5-48
"Butterfly wing effects, hand processed on glass:

RE 912-50
"Cosmos and Physalis"

RE 710-51

RE 710-52

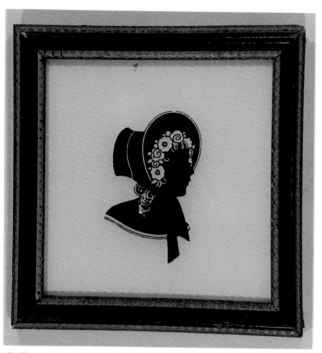

RE 44-61
"Colonial Girl"

RE 44-62
"Colonial Man"

RE 34-63
"A Fickle Wind"

RE 34-64
"Lucky April Shower"

46

RE 57-30
Unmarked

RE 45-31
"Southern Belle"
"Silver"

RE 45-32
"Southern Gentleman"
"Silver"

These pictures were also done with a cream color background.

RE 44-93

RE 44-94

"Another Reliance Product"

RE 44-83
"Courtship"

paired with

RE 44-84
"The Trysting Place"

RE 44-85

RE 44-87
"Spring in the Park"
paired with
"Sunshine and Shower"

RE 55-151
T-6
"The Gift Bearer" paired with "Sewing
Lesson."

– This is not painted on the glass.

– This silhouette is printed on paper.

RE 57-121
"Anticipation"
paired with
"Presentation"

RE 57-122
This type of silhouette is painted on the glass in black, then the cream color background is painted on. (See picture at top of next page for example of same silhouette with different background style.)

RE 57-123

The silhouette is painted on the glass in black, without painting a background. These pictures have a type of wrinkled, clear cellophane behind the glass.

RE 57-125
"Beau Brummel"

paired with

RE 57-126
"Lady Faire"

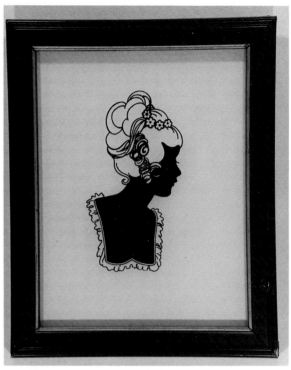

RE 45-65
"Lighthorse Harry Lee"   paired with   RE 45-66
"Sally Lee"

RE 57-127
"Home from School"
pairs with "Off to School"

RE 57-129
"Colonial Proposal"
pairs with "Colonial Courtship"

(The picture on the left is missing the cellophane)

RE 34-116
"Lantern Garden In Japan"
pairs with
"Tea Garden in Japan"

RE 34-118
"Tally Ho"
pairs with
"Honeymoon Departure"

RE 56-103
"Colonial Tea"
paired with
"Colonial Fireside"
This pair was also available in silver.

RE 57-70
"A Garden Romp"
paired with
"Garden Pastime"

RE 56-72
"T-1"

RE 57-74
Unmarked

RE 911-130
"Old Fashioned Courtship:
pairs with
"Promenade"

RE 911-132

RE 56-134
"T-1"

RE 56-108
"T-1"

RE 45-110
"T-3"

"Hand processed on glass" and each have NRA Stamp on them.

RE 45-112

"T-3"

"Hand Processed Glass"
and NRA Stamp

RE 45-114

"T-3"

"Homeward Bound" paired with
"Old Ironsides"

C & A Richards

C. & A. Richards was listed in the Boston City Directories between 1925 and 1960, originally as importers, and later as importers and manufacturers of pictures and frames. They were located at five different addresses over the years, with different owners:

1925   Alfons R. Richards and Charles R. Ostrowski
        220 Devonshire Street, Room 204
1930   72 Summer Street, 5th floor
1939   Richard Ostrowski
        275 Congress Street
1945   Charles Richards
1950   148 High Street

All in Boston, Mass.

Several of these pictures are signed "Eileen Virginia Dowd", in 1937. There was a commercial artist named Eileen V. Dowd, 9 Park, Room 23, R9, Atherstone, Dorchester (an area of Boston), listed in the directory in 1932, 1937, 1940, and 1945. The signatures (and sometimes the date) are in small letters near the outer edge of the picture, on the glass.

K.W. Diefenbach is another signature found on some of the pictures from C. & A. Richards. These are stamped "Made in Germany," but I do not know any of the dates. There is a reference to K. W. Diefenbach (1852-1914) in the book, *Silhouettes: A History and Dictionary of Artists,* by Mrs. E. Nevill Jackson.

Many companies made silhouettes in singles and pairs. C. & A. Richards most frequently made series of four and sometimes six. They were produced in a large variety of sizes and shapes.

RI 37-774
"Per Aspera Ad Astra"
by K. D. Diefenbach
Tallimit
C. & A. Richards
Boston, Mass."

RI 79-750

"Kinder Musik"
"by K. W. Diefenbach
A series of Four
'Tallimit Art'
C.A. Richards Boston, Mass
Reg. U.S.A. Pat Off."

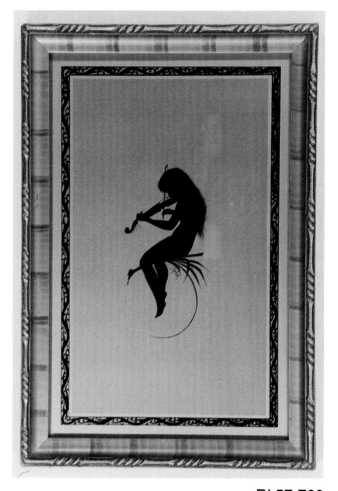

RI 57-760

"Elfin Music"
"by K. W. Diefenbach
A series of Four 'Tallimit Art'
C.A. Richards Boston, Mass"

RI 45-793

RI 45-795

"Rainbow Silhouettes" – "A series of Six by K.W. Diefenbach - 'Tallimit Art'
C & A Richards Boston, Mass."

RI 3½D-5187

RI 3½D-5186

"When Love Was Young" – "A Series of four - C. & A. Richards Boston, Mass."
I have seen this series with wood frames as well as the plastic shown above..

RI 5D-101

RI 5D-102

"Copyright 1937 - C & A Richards - signed Eileen Virginia Dowd"
The round frames shown above are black plastic with gold painted trim.

RI 44-592
"John Alden"
"C & A Richards Boston, Mass"

RI 4½x3½-5246
"The Old Heidelberg Inn Romancing"

The lower left silhouette was signed by Virginia Dowd and has a wood frame. It
has a tag from The Odd Shop owned by Dana Todd, in Minneapolis, Minnesota

RI 33½-5170

RI 33½-5169

RI 3½3½-314
"Minuets and Pierrettes"
"A series of four
© C & A Richards 1930"

RI 55-33
"Amourettes"
"A series of four
© C & A Richards 1931"

RI 35-720
"The Four Seasons
'Spring'
by
Fidus
C & A Richards Boston, Mass."

RI 45-5106
"Florals"
Hand Colored on Glass

RI 3½5½-474
"Somebody"
The silhouette on the right is shown
with the original box.

"Honey, May 19, '36"
was written on the back, in pencil
and it had apparently been tucked
away in a safe place for a least 50
years, since it is in mint condition!
The poem is © Emma E. Koehler

The last pages in this section have some of the examples which I have not been able to identify: some made by companies from which I have only two or three examples and very little information; examples of hand crafted silhouettes such as Tinsel Art. There are also examples of new silhouettes, dating from the 1970's and later (see page 80). These were included to show the differences between the older silhouettes and the new ones and have not been priced.

Examples of Tinsel Art

Tinsel art is a descriptive name given to this type of silhouette by collectors. These pictures are categorized together due to the similarity of the style and the fact that they are not done by a company, but by individuals.

The silhouettes are painted on the glass and crushed or crumpled tinfoil was used for a background. The glass is tinted on some examples. They can be found in many sizes, varied pictures, and occasionally they may be signed and dated.

This was apparently done by hobbyists and used in school art classes. I have spoken to several women who are in their seventies. They tell about going to school during the 1920's and learning to make silhouettes during school.

These examples were not professionally done, but are certainly interesting and quite charming. A few are even signed and dated. There seems to be an active interest in this style. They are priced higher at shows which specialize in primitive and country antiques and collectibles.

TA 810-7

TA 812-5
"painted by Mrs. P.A. Seely
1332 Avenue G, Fort Madison, Iowa"
signed on front "M. Seely"

TA 5½8-1

TA 810-3

TA 3½5½-10

TA 55-12
Signed R. Wagner, Written on the back in
fountain pen: "I hope you like this little
picture. It is handmade. Lil"

TA 810-8

TA 810-9

TA 57-14

TA 710-16

TA 58-18

TA 810-20

TA 9½12-22

TA 912-24

TA 1216-26

TA 911-28

67

The Photoplating Co.

215 N.E. 5th
Minneapolis, Minn.

The Photoplating Company was a manufacturer of advertising novelties. They produced silhouettes which bear a striking resemblance to modern day greeting cards. Those in my collection are dated 1932. They have verses and these examples are all directed to "Mother".

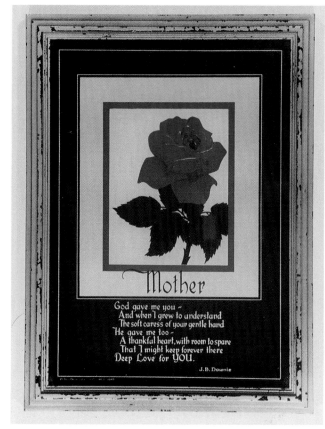

PH 57-51

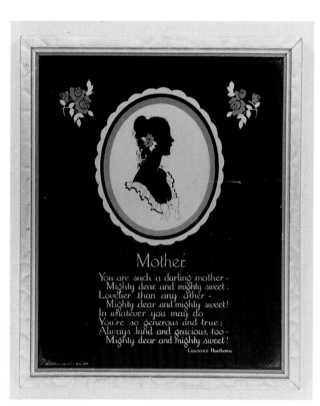

PH 78½-53
"Mother (Silhouette No. 53)
©The Photoplating Co., Mpls, 1932"

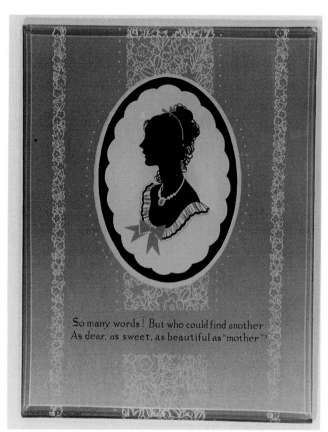

PH 4½6-52
©The Photoplating Co., Mpls, 1932"

68

P. F. Volland

Joliet, Ill.

A small company was started by J. Wallis, F. Clampitt, and P. Volland in 1908. This was a publishing company (making greeting cards) and first production was 20 mottoes made for framing.

The Volland Company has been out of business for about 35 years. They were purchased, along with several other companies, as subsidiaries of the parent company, United Printers & Publishers.

Some of the artists working for Volland were Janet Scott, Ella Brison, Catherine Sturgis and Frederick Richardson. Wilbur D. Nesbit was an extremely creative writer of verse and poem. The silhouette on the right has a poem written by Mr. Nesbit. It is quoted below.

Happiness
"Be happy!" sings the Bluebird.
"The world is full of smiles,
The sunshine always gleams
Above the little cloudy whiles."
The Bluebird makes it's Happiness –
It's song is meant to be
A cheery inspiration to such folk
As you and me.
– Wilbur D. Nesbit

VO 6½9-2
Artist signed: "Ellery Friend
© Volland"

VO 711-1
Artist signed: "Zula Kenyon
© Emma E. Koehler"

FR 912-5

FR 57-6

GG 56-3
"Gleam O'Gold Silhouettes
The Springtime of Life"

GO 57-120
"Chas. Gorman Art Studio
Chicago"

MF 9½12½-16
Unmarked

BP 812-1
"Manufactured by Baron Picture
Frameworks New York City"

SC 6½9½-3
"Hugo W. Schmidt Co. Detroit, Mich."

The West Coast Picture Company

Starting in 1929 the New York Picture Frame Company was established in Portland, at 500 Grand Ave. By 1931, they were listed at 1012 E. Broadway, with Plaquette Art Co. sharing the same address. The New York Picture Frame Co. is not listed after 1933 when the West Coast Picture Corp. started. Guy U. Tenney is the person who bought into a fledgling business, producing and selling pictures and frames.

The West Coast Picture Co., is still owned and operated by the Tenney family in Portland, Oregon.

WC 79-51
"West Coast Picture Corp.
3324 NE Broadway
Portland, Oregon"

WC 5½8-49
"Happy in her Garden manufactured by
Plaquette Art Co."

Picture #WC 5½8-49 would be from 1931 and Picture #WC 79-51 would have been after 1933 and before 1940, when the company moved to 2343 N.E. Holladay.

MF 710-1 dated "1920"   MF 710-2 dated "1920"

Color details and the silhouettes were reversed painted, then the cream colored background was painted over the entire back of the glass.

MF 79-3   MF 79-4

MF 2116-17

MF 2116-18

Both examples are signed by "Steinbrink" and are completely painted on glass except the background.

MF 45-19

MF 810-21
Signed on back "V.R. Cogs '32" Paper
is water stained and
tape frame is damaged.

MF 810-29
This is cut out.

MF 3D-25
"Guaranteed Vienna Handwork
Made in Austria"

MF 811-27

MF 610-23

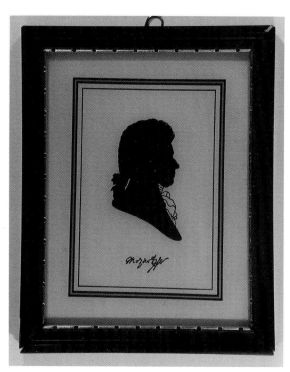

MF 56-31

MF 8½11-33
"Produced by the Long-Bell Lumber Co.,
Longview, Wn, U.S.A.
GrainArt Etchings in Wood"

MF 3½4½-35

MF 34-37

MF 68-39
This picture is ink on paper.

MF 7½12-41
This one is a cut out style.

MF 79½-43
The silhouette above is on printed paper, very old, and
was found at a flea market in Zurich, Switzerland.

The silhouettes below are in wood frames and painted on glass. Note the shadow in the background. This is due to a space between the glass and the background. They are all five inches in diameter.

RF 5D-3

RF 5D-5

RF 5D-7

RF 5D-8

RF 5D-9

RF 5D-11

FR 5D-13

RF 5D-15

MF 610-45

MF 510-47

BH 48-1

BH 48-2

Both lower examples have plastic frames and were made by Blaine Hudson Printing, Salt Lake City, Utah.

80

Lamp #1   Lamp #2   Lamp #3

Lamp #1 is marked "Perfume Hi-Lights by Stuart" and is 6" tall. Lamp #2 is 15" tall, the shade is 6" tall and 3" in diameter. Lamp #3 is marked "W" on the bottom and is 7½" tall.

Lamp #4 - Side view

Lamp #4 is 10" across and 8" tall. The silhouettes are painted on the front of the glass and the background is painted on the back, giving it a sunset appearance when lit.

Jewelry and Jewelry Boxes

Jewelry #2
This piece is 2⅛" diameter
and is black plastic on wood.

Jewelry #1
This pin is 1½" x 1½"
and the silhouette
is painted.

Jewelry Box #1
This box has a silhouette picture actually
set into the lid of the box.

Jewelry Box #2
This box is stamped on the bottom "Chromium
Plate Non Tarnishable"

Trays

Tray #1
This tray is 11" x 17"

Tray #2
This one is 4½" x 18"

Tray #3
This last tray is 8" x 12"

China and Miscellaneous

China #1 is marked on the back "Royal China - Warranted 22KT Gold". China #2 is a demitasse size cup and saucer, made by Salem China Co and the pattern name is 'Colonial'. China #3 contains several pieces: (a) ball water jug; (b) lamp; (c) water jug (d) tumblers. This appears to be a shape used by Universal Pottery, although the pieces are not marked.

China #1

China #2

China #3

This set is marked "Germany". My Grandmother had this same pattern over 30 years ago. I know they were old when she acquired them but she loved them and Grandpa built a special shelf for them. I found this set only two days after her funeral, and although they

were not hers, I could not leave the shop without buying them. Her set had four more pieces the size of the sugar and flour canisters. The oil and vinegar should have lids.

The tea set is marked "Germany". The photograph shows only two cups and saucers but this is a service for four.

The photographs at the left and the bottom left are a set. It is a mustard or small condiment, with a spoon, metal lid and an underplate. The lower right photograph is a mirror. The mirror magnifies and the handle is hard plastic with a joint, making it moveable.

Stamped on bottom "Made in England"

China #4

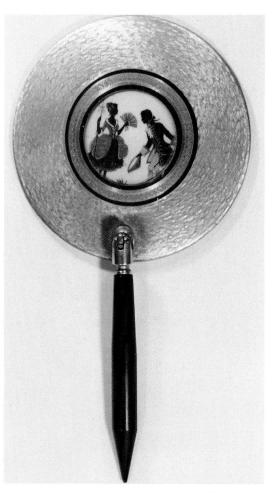

Mirror #1

The plate (China #5), is 8⅛" in diameter and is marked "Vilroy & Bach - Germany". The little pitcher was also made in Germany. The Harker plate (China #6) was made during the 1930's and the pattern is called 'Colonial Lady'. The ashtray (China #7) is one of a pair. The mate is the Washington Monument. The one pictured is George and Martha Washington and the ribbon underneath the silhouettes says "1732-1932".

China #5

China #6

China #7

China #8

Section Two

Convex Glass Silhouettes

The silhouettes on convex glass come in rectangular, oval and round shapes. The frames are made of metal, wood, plaster, celluloid, paper, or tape. The sizes range from 2½" x 3" oval to a 6" x 8" rectangle.

The most common sizes are 4" x 5" and 6" x 8". The most popular frames were of copper.

The silhouettes on the convex glass are hand painted or silk screened. The pictures were silk screened onto the glass and then the glass was heated to cause the convex shape. During this heating the paint was annealed to the glass making a very durable picture. There are a few examples of silhouettes where the background appears to have been air brushed. The hand painted silhouettes must be cleaned with great care since the paint will wash off. They are not annealed, but were apparently painted after the glass was shaped.

The backgrounds used in convex silhouettes are scenic or plain pink, blue, green and off-white textured paper. some of the background papers have pastel borders rather than scenic views.

The majority of the convex glass silhouettes are not marked. I have been able to identify the manufacturer in many cases by using salesman's samples, original boxes, and information from original price tags, etc.

As in section one, unmarked silhouettes are grouped with the marked and/or identified silhouettes to which they have the most similarity.

BA 45-1

Advertising Silhouettes
Baco Glass Plaque

These little pictures are painted on convex glass and were used as advertising gifts. The style of hanger or frame is shown on the Salesman sample, "Snowland Splendor". Notice the copyright date, "1950" in the corner of the picture. They were priced at 59 cents @ per lot of 100 or 51½ cents apiece, for orders of over 1,000. The background is marked on both of these examples: "Litho in the USA G Co."

Other advertising samples are shown in the section on Erickson (on the following two pages).

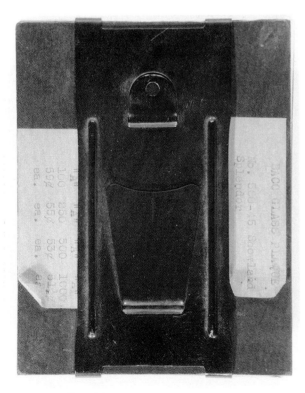

BA 45-2 (back)

BA 45-2 (front)
"Baco Glass Plaque"
"Snowland Splendor"

C. E. Erickson Co.

C. E. Erickson Co. (Claus E.), 1914-1974, were the years the company was listed and they were involved in various advertising specialties. I have pictures dated 1939, 1940, and 1941 with advertising. They have "Ericksons, Des Moines" on the background, right under the advertising. Some of the pictures have thermometers behind the convex glass. It has a simple, unpainted metal hanger, which could be bent to stand or hang.

ER 7D-7

ER 68-6
Painted on the glass, "© 1941"

ER57-5W

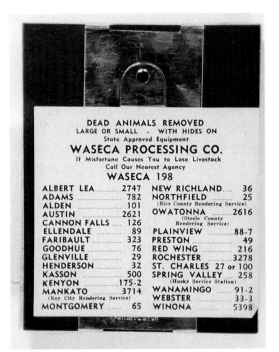

ER 45-1 (back)   ER 45-1B (front)

This is one which advertises for a company on the front and back. Marked
"Erickson, Des Moines - See other side" at bottom of picture.

ER 45-2   ER 45-3

Benton Glass Company

I had been collecting glass silhouette pictures for many years before I found the pair with a label on the back. See below for a photograph of the Salesman Sample, with the information about sizes, colors, and Behold!, the name of the company. We visited the Benton Harbor Public Library to find more information.

I found listings in the Polks Benton Harbor City Directory for Benton Glass Co. from 1940 to 1946. The owner was listed as Saul L. Colef, novelties manufacturers, at 280 Park. Saul Colef was a dentist and lived with his wife Sara, and two daughters at 988 Columbus Ave. and later at 1566 Miami Ave. Some of the pictures with the copyright "Copr. S. Colef" date from 1941 to 1945. Another example is with "© Benton Glass Co. R 185-17 Litho in U.S.A.". When these copyright notices are found, they are kind of hidden behind the painted silhouette. They are printed on the background. Most of the Benton silhouettes are not marked at all.

In October of 1946, Benton Glass Co. transferred its entire operation to 1407 E. 40th St., Cleveland, Ohio. The name was changed to Colef Glass Picture Company and later to Benton Glass Picture Co. Inc.

Benton Glass was a manufacturer of floral, landscape, baby, religious, and Mother's Day pictures. The most common sizes are 4" x 5" and 6" x 8". There are also some 3½" x 4½" and 5" x 7" sizes. Although the copper frames were very popular, plaster, wood, and other metals were used.

Trade names used were "Chrysto-Vex" pictures and "Plas-Stone" plaques. The pictures were sold in 5 & 10 cent variety stores, department stores and general mercantile stores. Benton Glass was reported out of business with no successor as of December 31, 1953.

Series No. 800

Size 6x8

Frame: copper

Description:
Black Silhouette over White
Blue Silhouette over White
Rose Silhouette over White
White Silhouette over Blue
White Silhouette over Pink

Boxed: one **PAIR** in fancy box

Pack: one doz. **PAIR** per carton

Assortment:
4 **PAIR** Black Silhouettes
2 **PAIR** Blue Silhouettes
2 **PAIR** Rose Silhouettes
4 **PAIR** White Silhouettes

Subjects: 6 **PAIR**

Weight: 16 lbs. per Carton

BENTON GLASS CO.
Benton Harbor, Michigan

BG 45-3

BG 45-4

BG 68-1W

BG 68-2W

BG 68-5R

BG 68-6R

BG 68-7B

BG 68-8B

BG 68-9

BG 68-10

BG 68-11

BG 68-12

BG 45-13

BG 45-14

BG 45-15

BG 45-16

BG 45-17

BG 45-18

BG 45-19

BG 45-20

BG 45-21

BG 45-22

BG 45-23

BG 45-24

BG 68-25

BG 68-26

BG 3½4½-27

BG 3½4½-28

BG 68-100
"This Little Piggy"
"Charlotte Becker"

BG 68-101

BG 68-102

BG 68-103

BG 68-104

BG 68-105

BG 68-106

BG 45-107

BG 45-108

BG 45-109

BG 45-110

BG 68-111

BG 68-112

BG 45-113

BG 45-114

BG 45-117

BG 45-118

BG 45-115

BG 45-116

BG 3½4½-119

BG 3½4½-120

BG 45-121

BG 45-122

BG 68-123

BG 68-124

BG 68-125

BG 68-126

BG 45-127
"©Benton Glass Co." "R185-15"

BG 45-128
"R-185-18"

Printed on both pictures "Litho in USA"

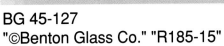

BG 68-129

BG 68-130

BG 45-131
"© Benton Glass Co" "R185-18"

BG 45-132
"© Benton Glass Co" "R185-17"

"Litho in USA"

BG 68-133

BG 68-134

" Copr. S. Colef 3-15-42"

BG 68-139
"© Morris & Bendien, NY"

BG 68-140
print signed "Sandre'"

BG 68-141

BG 68-142

"Copr. S. Colef 12-1-41" and signed "Roy"

BG 68-37 BG 68-38

BG 45-51 BG 45-52

Stamped on back of picture "Benton Glass Co."

110

BG 68-143

BG 68-144

These pictrues are stamped "1941, Donald Art Co., New York."
The white lace is painted on the convex glass.

BG 45-145

BG 45-146

BG 68-29

BG 68-30

BG 68-31

BG 68-32

BG 45-33

BG 45-34

BG 68-35

BG 68-36

BG 45-181

BG 45-182

BG 68-183

BG 68-184

BG 45-53

BG 45-54

"Copr S. Colef 5-1-45" is printed on both of these backgrounds.

BG 45-55

BG 45-56

BG 45-57

BG 45-58

BG 45-59

BG 45-60

BG 57-61

BG 57-62

BG 68-63

BG 68-64

BG 68-65

BG 68-66

BG 68-67

BG 68-68

BG 68-69

BG 68-70

BG 68-71

BG 68-72

BG 45-73

BG 45-74

"Copr "S. Colef 5-1-45" is on both of these background pictures.

BG 3½4½-75

BG 3½4½-76

BG 45-77

BG 45-78

BG 45-79

BG 45-80

BG 45-81

BG 45-82

BG 45-83

BG 45-84

BG 45-85

BG 45-86

BG 3½4½-87

BG 3½4½-88

BG 45-89   BG 45-90

BG 45-91   BG 45-92

This pair was received as a wedding gift in 1939.

The pictures on this page have a different set of identifiers put on by the manufacturer. I would certainly like to hear from anyone knowing anything about these marks as I was unable to find more information.

The picture on the left has "G 2800+ and "357" painted on the glass. It then has "GP 2800 1/2" and "Litho in USA" and "G Co", printed on the background.

The picture on the right has "G 3050" and "2058", painted on the glass. It then has "GP 3050" and "Litho in USA" and "G Co", printed on the background.

BG 45-151

BG 45-152

BG 45-153

BG 45-154

BG 45-155

BG 45-156

BG 45-157

BG 45-158

BG 45-159

BG 45-160

BG 45-161

BG 45-162

BG 45-163

BG 45-164

BG 45-165

BG 45-166

BG 3½4½-167

BG 3½4½-168

This is the very first pair of silhouettes I purchased, over 25 years ago. They were purchased in a second hand store in St. Paul, Minnesota. The properietor said, "I don't know what you want those for. They aren't antiques." I said, "I just like them". I have been buying them ever since!

BG 45-169

BG 45-170

BG 45-171

BG 45-172

BG 45-173

BG 45-174

BG 45-175R

BG 45-176R

The lower examples are exactly the same as the upper, except in red.

BG 45-177

BG 45-178

BG 68-179

BG 68-180

BG 45-181

BG 45-182

BG 68-183

BG 68-184

BG 45-185

BG 45-186

BG 45-187

BG 45-188

BG 45-191

BG 45-192

BG 3¹/₂4¹/₂-189

BG 3¹/₂4¹/₂-190

BG 68-193

BG 68-194

BG 68-195

BG 68-196

BG 68-197

BG 68-198

BG 68-199

BG 68-200

BG 45-201

BG 45-202

BG 45-203

BG 45-204

BG 45-205

BG 45-206

BG 45-207

BG 45-208

BG 45-209

BG 45-210

BG 45-211

BG 45-212

BG 45-213

BG 45-214

These two examples were found in the orginal, fancy box

BG 68-215

BG 68-216

These two are examples of the Plas-stone made by Benton Glass Co.

Bilderback's Inc.

The back of all three of these pictures have "A Handpainted Creation by Bilderback's Inc. of Detroit" on them.

The one on the right is 9 inches in diameter.

BI 9D-1

BI 6D-2

BI 6D-3

Edna Lewis Studio
Pequot Lakes, Minnesota

These examples are hand painted on curved glass and framed with a type of stick-on tape. Ms. Lewis was still painting these when I talked to her in the 1970's.

They all have a sticker on the back which says. "Edna Lewis Studios - Pequot Lakes, MN. Hand Painted".

LE 6D-1

LE 4½D-2

LE 4½D-3

Peter Watson's Studio

I have not been able to find where Peter Watson's studio was located. These are all signed "P.W." on the convex glass and most have the label on the back, as shown on the right.

PW 57-1 (Back)

PW 57-1

PW 57-2

PW 5D-3

PW 5D-4

PW 5D-5

PW 5D-6

PW 5D-7

PW 5D-8

PW 6D-9

PW 6D-10

PW 5D-11

PW 5D-12

PW 5D-13

PW 5D-14

Miscellaneous Silhouettes

The next five pages are filled with examples of miscellaneous silhouettes. These are pictures of silhouettes which did not fit into the categories of the other sections. They are also silhouettes for which I have not identified the manufacturer and/or do not have information or examples enough to make them worthy of a section of their own. Anyone with information to share, please contact me.

MC 5D-1

MC 9D-2

MC 5½D-3

MC 4D-4

MC 4D-5

MC 3½D-6

MC 3½D-7

MC 7D-11

MC 7D-12

MC 4D-13
"Hand Painted"

MC 4D-14
"Made in Czecho Slovakia"

MC 2½3½-15
Painted on clear celluloid with ivory celluloid frame.

MC 46-16

MC 45-17
"Made in USA F.T.S. 104
Hand Painted Price $1.80"

OH 45-1
"Made in USA
Ohio Art Co."

WP 4½5-1

WP 4½5-2

Just for variety, I am including the photographs of a pair of wall pockets. The edges are sealed with black tape which has started to fray.

DeMAS
JEWELRY
Finest Optical Service
Successor to DeLorenzo Bros.
2647 Gratiot   Detroit, Mich.
Tel. Fitzroy 5088

MC 57-18

1992
Price Guide
for

Encyclopedia of

On Glass

by
Shirley Mace

Section One
Flat Glass Values

Section Two
Convex Glass Values